Author: Grandpa Tom Hayden
Illustrations by: Laurie Burrill Renecker

HAYDEN BURRILL
FIRST EDITION   JUNE 1985

Copyright© 1984 by Tom Hayden Enterprises
Published by Tom Hayden Enterprises
2999 Twin Oaks Place N.W.
Salem, Oregon 97304

ISBN 0-9613969-1-1

To Mitzy my wife
who loves me
just the way I am.

Upon a time once, Melissa Muldune, age twelve, lived in the deep south of the country in a town called Imagineville, U.S.A.

Melissa's daddy was Major Muldune, a retired horse owner-racer who had made quite a name for himself racing, fighting duels in the name of honor, and dancing with all the pretty girls. When he was young, of course.

Melissa had a rich grandma whose heritage dated back as far as Adam and Eve (on the wealthy side). Though filthy rich, Grandma Magnolia Muldune was a grand old gal. She was raising Melissa as Melissa's mama died when Melissa was only four.

Major Muldune owned a twenty-five-year-old horse named "Charles the III," who, during his racing career, had won the "Kentucky Fried Derby" as a three-year-old. Charles then was retired to become a papa horse in order to continue his line of super-fast race horses. At twenty-five he became Melissa's horse — as she loved him very much.

Melissa nicknamed him Charlie. He loved carrots, sugar, clover – and most of all, standing still! When riding time came he'd pretend he had a cramp in his left hind leg, and he'd make it twitch. If that didn't work, he would limp. If that didn't work, he'd lie on his back with all four legs in the air, close his eyes and stop breathing. When that failed to fool Melissa, they went riding.

From the way Charlie carried on, it may sound like Melissa didn't get to ride very often, but she did since she was more persistent than Charlie was stubborn. Charlie was pretty fast on occasion (for a twenty-five-year-old horse!) but going downhill he was REALLY FAST!!

Melissa had a friend from school named Bobby Break. They had become good friends because they both loved horses. Bobby's folks didn't have much money and he wasn't lucky enough to have his own horse. Melissa shared Charlie with Bobby, who lived one mile and twenty-seven feet from Major Muldune's mansion.

One day, after pulling Charlie out of the barn on his back and pushing him up the hill, they had a fun, fast ride down the old hill behind the mansion. Bobby said, "I've got an idea! If it works, we could win the County Fair kid's horserace on Charlie, and get the 1st place trophy!!"

As they headed for the barn, Bobby explained to Melissa, "If we raise Charlie's back hooves so that his hind end is higher than his front, Charlie will think he is going down hill. Then he'll go as fast as he does when he is going downhill!!" Melissa was thrilled. "What a great idea," she said, "but how are you going to do it?"

"Easy," said Bobby, "My dad's uncle Boom Boom is a blacksmith. I'm sure he will make us some special platform shoes for Charlie's back hooves." And with this great plan the kids pulled off Charlie's saddle and bridle, gave him some sugar, and ran into the house to have some of Grandma Magnolia's cookies and milk.

Well, the kids got Charlie entered into the Race much to the surprise of Major Muldune. He was sure that his old "Charles the III" was a kid's horse, <u>not</u> a 25-year-old County Fair Race horse named Charlie.

The night before the big race, Charlie was introduced to his new platform racing shoes at Boom Boom the Blacksmith's. Charlie thought they felt pretty good and he noticed that he even had a tendency to walk faster (to keep from falling forward on his nose!).

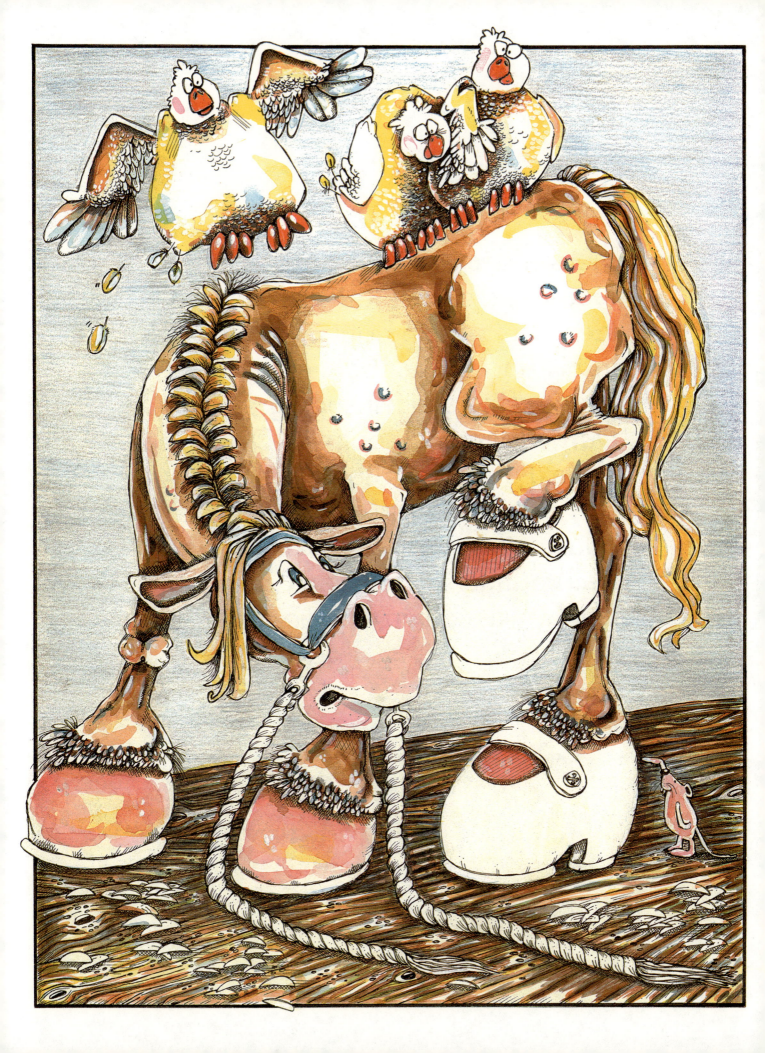

Melissa decided that Bobby should race Charlie since the shoes were his idea. And I mean Bobby looked great in his Racing Rainbow colors. They were racing against such greats as Dunsenberry – Spootnik – Dead Heat – Cold Turkey – Stomach Pump – Hot Pistol – Bent MaMa – and the odds-on favorite, Gone with the Wind – all younger horses than Charlie; but Bobby was certain Charlie could win.

"THEY'RE OFF" – Charlie, in order to keep from falling on his nose, fell into the lead to gain a ½ length on the other horses. His speed was mind-boggling. He went faster and faster, just to keep from falling on his nose!!!

Charlie felt like the young "Charles the III" and really started pouring it on, leaving the other horses behind in the dust. Well, Major Muldune was astounded. Magnolia was in a state of shock, and Melissa was screaming "COME ON CHARLIEEEEEEEE!!"

WHEN SUDDENLY —

Both Charlie's back legs cramped and locked up. He skidded to a stop on his nose, and fell over on his side. As the other horses galloped by, Charlie felt he had let Bobby and Melissa down by not winning the race. If you had been close, you would have seen the tears in his eyes.

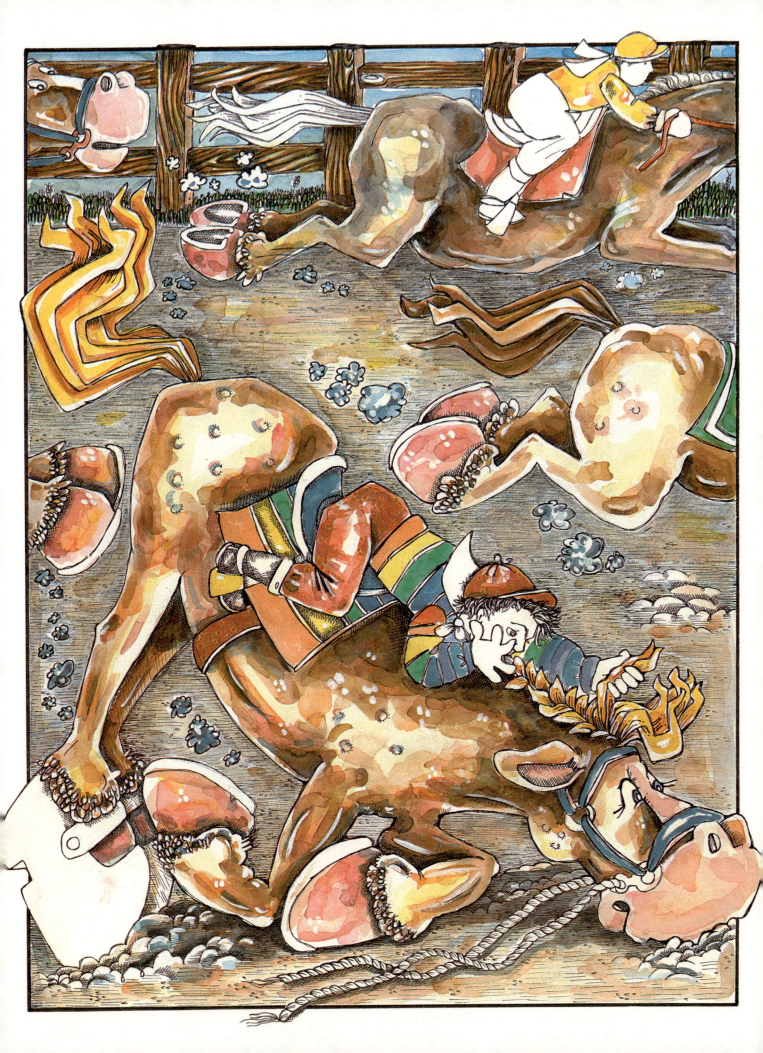

Charlie couldn't move, so they placed
him carefully in the back of a truck.
They took him home where they
laid him on some straw in the stable.
Bobby felt just terrible because the
shoes were his idea. Charlie wouldn't
even eat; nor would he even look at
his friends, Bobby and Melissa.

"If you don't get Charlie on his hooves and eating in the next couple of days," Major Muldune said quietly, "you'll lose him." Magnolia fainted. Bobby felt tears coming to his eyes – and Major Muldune had a lump in his throat. Melissa kneeled down and –

Whispered in Charlie's ear, *"Charlie, I love you just the way you are."* With that, Charlie's eyes blinked a couple of times, and blinked again, and then they stayed open.

Charlie felt so much better. He got to his hooves realizing that winning the race wasn't as important as having Melissa and Bobby love him for what he was – an old (but charming) kid's horse.

Need I tell you, they all lived happily ever after. Melissa and Bobby rode Charlie all around the old Plantation and Charlie thought to himself, "I bet in years to come, they'll call a terrible cramp like that – A CHARLIE HORSE! – in honor of me – of course!!"

This Book Belongs to:

_____

Dear Friend,
    Thank you for buying this book and becoming an official member of Charlie's Fan Club.

On the opposite page is an official picture that you may cut out and color.